"The Puritan William Gurnall once said, 'Prayer is nothing but the promise reversed or God's word turned inside out and formed into an argument and retorted back again upon God by faith.' It sounds great. But what does it look like in practice? *5 Things to Pray for the People You Love* and *5 Things to Pray for Your Church* answer that question. They'll walk you through using God's word in prayer. And praying God's word is my number one tip to help people invigorate their prayer life. Read these books and invigorate your prayers."

Tim Chester, Pastor of Grace Church, Boroughbridge, and author of *You Can Pray* (IVP)

"*Five Things to Pray* is a brilliantly simple but hugely effective means of stimulating your prayer life for church, mission, family and friends. Accessible and attractive, with lots of Scripture to focus prayer, it will be a great tool for churches to help members to pray regularly and creatively."

Trevor Archer, FIEC Training Director

"I recommend this series to you on the basis of the simple fact that they moved me to pray. They both showed me ways to pray for my church and my loved ones, and they kindled in my heart a *want* to pray. These are simple books, with the modest and eternally profound aim of showing how the Bible informs our prayers. Rachel Jones manages to withdraw from the picture and leaves the reader to see how simple it is to align our prayers with the will of our listening Father. These books could well be a cause of great blessing for your church and people you love."

John Hindley, Pastor of BroadGrace Church, Norfolk, and author of *Serving Without Sinking* and *You Can Really Grow*

"For those of us who often struggle to know what to pray for our church and for the people we love, these books are brilliant at giving us lots of really helpful, specific things to pray that are straight from God's word. With a mixture of praise, confession, thanksgiving and petition, the prayers are repeatedly focused on what it looks like to live in the light of eternity in the various different situations that are highlighted. Starting with Scripture really helpfully ensures that we are not praying merely for changed circumstances, as we can tend to do, but rather for changed hearts that bring honour and glory to God."

Andrea Trevenna, Associate Minister for Women at St Nicholas, Sevenoaks, and author of *The Heart of Singleness*

FOR THE PEOPLE YOU LOVE

RACHEL JONES

SERIES EDITOR: CARL LAFERTON

5 things to pray for the people you love
Prayers that change things for your friends and family
© The Good Book Company, 2016
Reprinted 2016 (twice), 2017.
Series Editor: Carl Laferton

Published by
The Good Book Company
Tel (UK): 0333 123 0880
Tel (North America): (1) 866 244 2165
International: +44 (0) 208 942 0880
Email (UK): info@thegoodbook.co.uk
Email (North America): info@thegoodbook.com

Websites
UK & Europe: www.thegoodbook.co.uk
North America: www.thegoodbook.com
Australia: www.thegoodbook.com.au
New Zealand: www.thegoodbook.co.nz

ISBN: 9781910307397 | Printed in Denmark

Design by André Parker

CONTENTS

INTRODUCTION

I wonder if you have ever struggled to believe this famous verse from the Bible:

> *"The prayer of a righteous person is powerful and effective" (James 5 v 16).*

James is telling us that when righteous people pray righteous prayers, things happen. Things change. The prayers of God's people are powerful. But they are not powerful because we are powerful, or because the words we say are somehow magic, but because the Person we pray to is infinitely, unimaginably powerful. And our prayers are effective—not because we are special, or because there is a special formula to use, but because the God we pray to delights to answer our prayers and change the world because of them.

So what is the secret of effective prayer—how can you pray prayers that really change things? James suggests two questions that we need to ask ourselves.

First, are you righteous? A righteous person is some-one who is in right relationship with God—someone who, through faith in Jesus, has been forgiven and accepted as a child of God. Are you someone who,

yes

as you pray, is praying not just to your Maker, not just to your Ruler, but to your heavenly Father, who has completely forgiven you through Jesus?

Second, do your prayers reflect that relationship? If we know God is our Maker, our Ruler and our Father, we will want to pray prayers that please him, that reflect his desires, that line up with his priorities for our lives and for the world. The kind of prayer that truly changes things is the prayer offered by a child of God that reflects God's heart.

That's why, when God's children pray in the Bible, we so often find them using the word of God to guide their prayers. So when Jonah prayed in the belly of a fish to thank God for rescuing him (Jonah 2 v 1-9), he used the words of several psalms strung together. When the first Christians gathered in Jerusalem to pray, they used the themes of Psalm 2 to guide their praise and their requests (Acts 4 v 24-30). And when Paul prayed that his friends would grow in love (Philippians 1 v 9), he was asking the Father to work in them the same thing the Lord Jesus prayed for us (John 17 v 25-26), and which the Holy Spirit is doing for all believers (Romans 5 v 5). They all used God's words to guide their words to God.

How can you pray prayers that are powerful and effective—that change things, that make things happen? First, by being a child of God. Second, by praying Bible prayers, which use God's words to make sure your prayers are pleasing to him and share his priorities.

That's what this little book is here to help you with. It contains suggestions for how to pray for 21 different kinds of people you know and love. And for each of them you'll find guidance for what we can pray for them—for parents, for children, for those who are sick, for those who are seeking, for those who have just been born and about those who have just died, and many more. Each prayer suggestion is based on a passage of the Bible, so you can be certain that they are prayers that God wants you to pray for your loved ones.

There are five different suggestions for each. So you can use this book in a variety of ways.

- *You can pray a prayer each day for a loved one, over the course of three weeks, and then start again.*

- *You can take one of the prayer themes and pray a part of it every day from Monday to Friday.*

- *Or you can dip in and out of it, as and when you want and need to pray for a loved one in a particular circumstance.*

- *There's also a space on each page for you to write in the names of the people you are praying for regularly.*

This is by no means an exhaustive guide—there are plenty more things that you can be praying for your friends and relatives! But you can be confident as you use it that you are praying great prayers—prayers that God wants you to pray. And God promises that "the prayer of a righteous person is powerful and effective". That's a promise that is worth grasping hold of confidently. As we pray trusting this promise, it will change how we pray and what we expect to come from our prayers.

When righteous people pray righteous prayers, things happen. Things change. So as you use this book to guide your prayers, be excited, be expectant, and keep your eyes open for God to do "immeasurably more than all we ask or imagine" (Ephesians 3 v 20). He's powerful; and so your prayers are too.

Carl Laferton
Editorial Director
The Good Book Company

A CHRISTIAN PARENT

DEUTERONOMY 6 v 1-9

Gary, kids, family, Gina, Hudson, myself, Lee + Sally, Pam, Tony

THANK GOD FOR FAMILIES

> *"… so that you, your children and their children after them may fear the LORD your God … and so … enjoy long life" (v 2).*

Time and again in the Old Testament, God chooses to deal with families, not individuals. Praise God that family matters to him. Then thank him for this particular family and for the life that they share together.

Then pray that this parent would enjoy…

A LOVE FOR GOD

> *"Love the LORD your God with all your heart and with all your soul and with all your strength" (v 5).*

It's God, not our children, who should occupy first position in our hearts. Pray that this parent would resist the temptation to turn their child into an idol. And pray that their love for God would be teaching their child an important but counterintuitive lesson: *You're not the centre of the universe.*

FOCUS ON GOD'S COMMANDS

> *"These commandments that I give you today are to be on your hearts" (v 5).*

Pray that this parent would keep God's commands on their heart and in their head through the day—his call to be <u>loving</u>, <u>patient</u>, <u>selfless</u>, truthful, <u>gentle</u>, <u>self-controlled</u>, <u>forgiving</u> and <u>repentant</u>. Pray that these qualities would make a difference to the way they parent, in all the mundane busyness: the school run, washing up, disciplining, bathtime, sports practice…

 TIME TO TEACH

> *"Impress them on your children. Talk about them when you sit at home…" (v 7).*

Pray that this parent would appreciate that their greatest responsibility to their child is not securing them a good education or developing their talents, but teaching them about Jesus. Ask God to help this family to start—or sustain—regular times of reading the Bible and praying together.

 WHOLE-LIFE DEVOTION

> *"… and when you walk along the road" (v 7).*

Pray that this parent would find creative ways to bring Jesus into all aspects of family life. It can be easy to give the impression that God is only for Sunday mornings: but pray that this parent would display the truth that all of life belongs to God, and every moment can be used to enjoy and worship him.

A WIFE

PROVERBS 31 v 10-31

PEOPLE TO PRAY FOR:

 PRAISE GOD

"A woman who fears the LORD is to be praised" (v 30).

If this woman is a Christian, praise God for her faith! Pray that she would live in awe of her God's power, authority and love. If she isn't yet a Christian, ask God to put a fear of him in this woman's heart; that she would come to see that she is facing God's judgment, but is able to enjoy God's mercy in Christ.

Then ask God to give this woman...

 A STRONG MARRIAGE

"She brings [her husband] good, not harm, all the days of her life" (v 12).

Pray for this woman's relationship with her husband; ask God to help her selflessly to seek his good. Pray that God would be working in this marriage to strengthen and mature it. Pray through any specific pressure points, disappointments or sources of hurt that you are aware of.

3 A GENEROUS HEART

"She opens her arms to the poor and extends her hands to the needy" (v 20).

Pray that this woman would be generous with her time and resources. In a culture that tells us to look after "you and yours" first, it's very easy to become inward looking in our concerns. Pray that this wife would have arms that are open and a heart that is ready to love; that she would be ready to bring into her family those who are lonely and in need.

4 WISE SPEECH

Pray that she would be a woman who "speaks with wisdom" (v 26).

Ask our Father to fill her mouth with sound advice, gentle rebukes, cheerful encouragements and grateful thanks. And ask him to guard her lips against words that are resentful, complaining, gossiping or hurtful.

5 BLESSED FAMILY LIFE

"Her children arise and call her blessed; her husband also" (v 28).

Pray for this woman's husband and any children she has. Pray that they would notice and appreciate all she does for them, and would know how to encourage and thank her.

A HUSBAND

JOSHUA 1 v 1-9

PEOPLE TO PRAY FOR:

Gary, Nate, Jeff, Erik

As you bring this man before God, pray for…

1 COURAGEOUS LEADERSHIP

> *"Be strong and courageous, because you will lead these people…" (v 6).*

As Joshua was chosen to lead God's people towards the promised land, so God gives husbands the job of leading their family towards the promised heavenly country. Pray that this man would lead his family faithfully towards eternity—or pray that he would discover for himself for the first time the wonderful promise of eternal life.

2 OBEDIENCE TO GOD'S WORD

> *"Be careful to obey all the law" (v 7).*

Obeying God, and leading others to do that, takes conscious care. Pray that this man would not only read God's word, but would remember and deliberately act on it. And pray that he would not use obedience in one area as an excuse for ignoring God's commands in another part of his life. Pray about any areas where you know he is struggling at the moment.

communication

illness
patience

GOD-HONOURING SPEECH

> *"Keep this Book of the Law always on your lips" (v 8).*

Pray that all this man's speech to his wife would honour God; and always be loving, encouraging and truthful, and never thoughtless or angry. Pray that he would be building up his wife's faith by reminding her of truths from God's word.

 TRANSFORMATION BY GOD'S WORD

> *"... meditate on it day and night" (v 8).*

Pray that this man would be devoted to reading God's word and hearing it taught. Pray that he wouldn't just hear God's word, but would meditate on it; that God would plant his truth deep into this man's heart, transforming his character and behaviour to be more Christ-like.

 THE RIGHT RESPONSE TO DISCOURAGEMENT

> *"Do not be discouraged; for the LORD your God will be with you wherever you go" (v 9).*

Disappointments can so easily breed resentment or resignation. Pray that this husband would not allow setbacks, difficult circumstances or his own flaws to stop him leading his family in a Christ-like way. Pray that when discouragement comes, he would be able to see God at work in and through it.

A BABY

**EPHESIANS 1 v 18-19;
6 v 4, 19-20**

PEOPLE TO PRAY FOR:

Quinn, Julia, Jacob, Scarlett

 FAITH IN CHRIST

*"I pray that the eyes of your heart may be
enlightened in order that you may know the
hope to which he has called you…" (1 v 18).*

More than anything else, this baby needs to know the
certain, eternal hope of a future with Christ. This is
the most important thing you can pray for them. You
probably know this, but it's so very easy to pray for
health/happiness/a good night's sleep instead.

 CHURCH MEMBERSHIP

*"… the riches of his glorious inheritance in
his holy people" (v 18).*

This baby needs a church, and will do every day from
their first to their last, so that they will grow up knowing saints of all ages who will show and teach them
about their inheritance. Pray that as this baby grows
up, they would be part of a fellowship that helps their
parents to love, model grace, do godly discipline,
and enjoy being together as God's people.

GOD'S POWER

> "... and his incomparably great power for
> us who believe" (v 19).

If God blesses this child by granting the above two requests, they will have a hard life: fighting the internal battle of sin, and suffering the external persecution of a world which does not know Christ. Pray that God would be strengthening and changing this child even as they lie in their cot.

 GODLY PARENTS

> "Fathers, do not exasperate your children;
> instead bring them up in the training and
> instruction of the Lord" (6 v 4).

Fathers, and mothers, need spiritual help to do this. Pray that they wouldn't do what's easiest for them; wouldn't lay down unnecessary rules; wouldn't be inconsistent; wouldn't ever let there be a gap between what they tell this child about Christ, and how they live for him; wouldn't ever act as though this child most needs good behaviour or good grades.

 THE PRIVILEGE OF SUFFERING

> "I am an ambassador in chains" (v 20).

Don't pray that God would bless this child with a long life, a successful life or a respected life. Pray that a million years from now, this child would be known for how he/she lay down their dreams, comforts, health, and even their life to serve Christ.

A SCHOOL
CHILD

JAMES 1 v 17-21

PEOPLE TO PRAY FOR:

_____

_____

_____

_____

 GIVE THANKS

"Every good and perfect gift is from above" (v 17).

Give thanks for this child, for the gift from God that they are—for their unique personality, talents and interests. And pray that they would grow in thankfulness to God, not taking the good things they have and enjoy for granted.

 FAITH THROUGH GOD'S WORD

"He chose to give us birth through the word of truth…" (v 18).

Thank God that there is a word more precious than any of the ones taught in school. Thank God that he gives new life through faith in his Son, who we meet in his word. Pray that this child will come to faith, or grow in faith, this year—and pray that their parents and family would want this for them more than any educational achievements or qualifications.

DISTINCTIVE LIVING

"… that we might be a kind of firstfruits of all he created" (v 18).

Pray that this child would speak and act differently to those around them at school, because they belong to God's new creation. Pray that in them, others would see how great it is to know Jesus. Pray that they would be willing to stand out, and if necessary to miss out, in order to live as part of God's people.

 CARING LISTENER

"Everyone should be quick to listen, slow to speak and slow to become angry" (v 19).

Pray that this child: would be a caring listener to classmates, noticing those who are hurting or lonely; would speak words which point to Jesus, not to themselves; would respond to being wronged with love and forgiveness, not anger and revenge.

 SHAPED BY THE WORD

"Get rid of all moral filth and the evil that is so prevalent, and humbly accept the word" (v 21).

Pray that the word would have more influence on this child than the world. And pray that they would not believe the lies of the world—either the obvious ones ("Your happiness is all-important", "Porn is harmless", and so on) or the less obvious ones ("Good grades are all-important", "If you work hard and obey well, then you are a good person").

A TEENAGER

DANIEL 1

PEOPLE TO PRAY FOR:

_____

_____

_____

_____

Father, please grant this teenager...

CITIZENSHIP OF HEAVEN

"Then the king ordered Ashpenaz, chief of his court officials, to bring into the king's service some of the Israelites" (v 3).

Just as God's people were aliens in Babylon, pray that this teenager would see themselves as a foreigner in this world, but a citizen of heaven. As they begin to make decisions that will affect the direction of their life, pray that they would want to spend it working for the kingdom of heaven before any earthly employer.

FIRM RESOLVE

"Daniel resolved not to defile himself" (v 8).

Pray that this teenager would show the same resolve as Daniel—resisting the pressure to do what is wrong. As their peers and the media call on them to conform to "normal" teenage behaviour—be that gossip, sex or drunkenness—pray that this teenager would stand up for what's right and be prepared to live a life that's distinctively different.

3 GOOD HEALTH

"Healthier and better nourished..." (v 15).

Teenage years bring raging hormones, changing bodies and insatiable appetites. Pray that God would be keeping this young person physically and mentally healthy as they grow.

 ### **4 KNOWLEDGE AND UNDER-STANDING**

Pray that God would give this young person "knowledge and understanding of all kinds of literature and learning" (v 17).

Pray for this teenager in their studies—that they would have a good attitude which honours God, being eager and willing to learn. Pray that they would respect their teachers in the way that they behave. And pray that they would work hard to make the most of the gifts that God has given them.

 ### **5 TRUE WISDOM**

Pray that God would give this teenager true "wisdom" (v 20).

Ask God to give this teenager a deep love for God's word, and a real desire to apply it to their life. Wherever this teenager stands in their faith right now, pray that God would increase their wisdom "ten times" over.

AN OLDER PERSON

PHILIPPIANS 4 v 4-9

PEOPLE TO PRAY FOR:

_____

_____

_____

_____

Father, please help this person to...

 REJOICE

"Rejoice in the Lord always" (v 4).

Old age can bring new, or more serious, difficulties: ill-health, bereavement, loneliness, financial concerns. Pray that through all this, this person would discover—or grow in—the joy of knowing they have a Saviour. Pray that this season of life would not bring cynicism, judgmentalism or regret. Pray instead for an increasing joy in the presence of Christ and the prospect of heaven.

 RESIST ANXIETY

Pray that this person would "not be anxious about anything, but [would] present [their] requests to God" (v 6).

Bring before God some of the specific issues that are worrying them at the moment. Then ask that "in every situation", they would be relying on God in prayer, and fighting the temptation to be anxious.

ENJOY GOD'S PEACE

"And the peace of God ... will guard your hearts and minds in Christ Jesus" (v 7).

If this person isn't a Christian, ask God to bring them to faith, so that through the work of Jesus Christ they would have peace with God—and with it, peace in other aspects of their life too. If they are a Christian, pray that the peace of God would fill their hearts and minds even in troubling circumstances.

 THINK POSITIVELY

Pray that your loved one's mind would be filled with things that are "true ... noble ... right ... pure ... lovely ... admirable ... excellent [and] praiseworthy" (v 8).

Pray that they would be able to resist the temptation to be negative, critical and complaining, but instead enjoy a positive outlook.

 APPLY GOD'S WORD

"Whatever you have learned ... put it into practice" (v 9).

Thank God for this person's wealth of wisdom and life experience. Pray that even if they feel that most of life is behind them, they wouldn't give up on striving to be more and more godly. Pray instead that they would be seeking every day to apply God's word to their life.

A NEIGHBOUR

ACTS 17 v 16-34

PEOPLE TO PRAY FOR:

_____

_____

_____

_____

Father God, please cause this person to...

BE CURIOUS

"You are bringing some strange ideas to our ears, and we would like to know what they mean" (v 20).

Christianity is probably "strange ideas" to your neighbour; perhaps they're confused about what it's all about, or they have heard unhelpful things from the media, or even another Christian. Pray that, despite these misconceptions, your neighbour would be curious about your faith and want to know more.

BE DISSATISFIED WITH WORLDLY THINGS

"You are ignorant of the very thing you worship" (v 23).

What is your neighbour worshipping? Their children? Their career? Their football team? Pray that your neighbour would become dissatisfied with chasing after these things and start searching for a life with real meaning.

BE PART OF YOUR PLAN

> *"[God] marked out their appointed times in history and the boundaries of their land" (v 26).*

God has planned that you and your neighbour would live in the same place at the same time; reflect on that and be excited! Then ask that God would use you in playing out his sovereign purposes.

 SEEK YOU

> *Pray that your neighbour would "seek [God] and perhaps reach out for him and find him" (v 27).*

What might "seeking God" look like for your neighbour? Coming to church or an evangelistic event? Reading the Bible or a Christian book? Asking you about your faith over a meal at your house? However it might happen, pray for opportunities for your neighbour to hear the gospel from you.

 RESPOND WITH BELIEF

> *Pray that they would not "sneer", but would want to "hear you again on this subject" (and again… and again… and again…).*

Pray that in time, they would come to believe the good news (v 32-34). Pray that God would give you patience and perseverance to keep faithfully sharing the gospel, however long it takes.

A COLLEAGUE

COLOSSIANS 3 v 22 – 4 v 6

PEOPLE TO PRAY FOR:

_____

_____

_____

_____

 A TRANSFORMED ATTITUDE

First, pray that you would work well, not only when your boss's "eye is on you ... but with sincerity of heart and reverence for the Lord. Whatever you do, work at it with all your heart" (3 v 22-23).

This is a tall order! We can only do it by the Holy Spirit—invite him to transform your attitude to work. Then pray that your countercultural way of working would grab the attention of your non-Christian colleague.

 SPIRITUAL HUNGER

"You know that you will receive an inheritance from the Lord as a reward" (v 24).

Thank God that you aren't slaving for a bigger house, a flashier car or a more exotic holiday; that instead, you can look forward to treasure in heaven that will never run out or disappoint. Pray that your colleague would become dissatisfied with their financial rewards and big promotions, and instead be searching for something that will last for ever.

 **GOD'S GRACE**

"Anyone who does wrong will be repaid for their wrongs" (v 25).

Thank God that Jesus has paid the price for your wrongdoing. Then ask him to extend his grace to this work friend, who so desperately needs it.

 GOSPEL OPPORTUNITIES

Pray that God "may open a door for our message, so that [you] may proclaim the mystery of Christ" (4 v 3).

Pray that he would provide situations that allow you to share the gospel with your colleague. Pray that you'd be ready to "make the most of every opportunity" (v 5). Ask God to help you speak "clearly" (v 4)—keeping the fundamentals in focus and finding just the right words to use.

 SALTY SPEECH

Pray that your conversations at work would "be always full of grace, seasoned with salt" (v 6).

Think about some of the situations when you find this difficult: when office politics get messy, when the banter gets crude or when deadlines are looming. Pray that your speech would be salty—distinctively different from that of your colleagues. Pray that you'd be able to show each person you work with the same undeserved grace that God has shown you.

A NON-CHRISTIAN FRIEND WHO IS SEARCHING

ACTS 8 v 26-39

PEOPLE TO PRAY FOR:

Father, grant that this friend would...

LOOK IN THE RIGHT PLACE

> *"This man ... was sitting in his chariot reading the Book of Isaiah" (v 27-28).*

Thank God for your friend's interest in spiritual things, even if they do not yet fully understand. There are lots of things that claim to be able to connect people to "God"—but in reality there is only one way we can know him. Pray that, like the Ethiopian man in Acts 8, your friend would begin to look in the right place for answers—the Bible.

BE GIVEN OPPORTUNITIES

> *"'Do you understand what you are reading?' Philip asked" (v 30).*

Pray that God would help you to take the initiative in turning conversations towards Jesus. Ask God to provide you with unmissable opportunities like Philip's—and that you would take them!

HEAR THE GOOD NEWS

"[Philip] told him the good news about Jesus" (v 35).

Thank God that the truth about Jesus really is wonderfully good news! Spend some time reflecting on God's grace in the gospel. Then pray that you would get a chance to talk with your friend not just about church life or different issues—but about the person at heart of the gospel: Jesus Christ.

 ## MAKE A COMMITMENT

Pray that, like the Ethiopian, your friend would come to the point where they say: "What can stand in the way of my being baptised?" (v 36).

So often people can hear the facts about Jesus, acknowledge them as true, and yet be unwilling to commit to following him. What might be standing in the way of your friend nailing their colours to the mast and becoming a Christian? (Their money? Their partner? A fear of what other people would think?) Ask God to miraculously remove these obstacles, or empower your friend to overcome them.

 ## REJOICE

"[He] went on his way rejoicing" (v 39).

Pray that by trusting in Jesus, your friend would find true, eternal joy. Ask that one day, their faith would bring great joy to God's people—yourself included.

A NON-CHRISTIAN
FRIEND WHO
SEEMS HOSTILE

1 PETER 3 v 13-18

PEOPLE TO PRAY FOR:

_____

_____

_____

_____

Lift this friend up to God and pray...

 ## FOR COURAGE

> *"'Do not fear their threats; do not be fright-
> ened.' But in your hearts revere Christ as
> Lord" (v 14-15).*

Pray that you would not fear indignant words, odd
looks or awkward silences. Instead, pray that you
would treat Christ as Lord, and that you would seek
his glory above your own comfort. Confess those
times when, out of fear, you have dodged an opportunity to defend Jesus in front of this friend. Pray for
courage when these opportunities come up again.

 ## FOR QUESTIONS & ANSWERS

> *Pray that you would "always be prepared
> to give an answer to everyone who asks
> you to give the reason for the hope that
> you have" (v 15).*

Pray that this friend would ask that question! And pray
that when they do, God would give you the words to
speak clearly and rationally.

FOR AWARENESS OF SIN

> Pray that "those who speak maliciously against your good behaviour in Christ may be ashamed of their slander" (v 16).

Pray that your words and behaviour would be so gracious that your friend would feel ashamed of the way they have spoken about Jesus. Pray that God would give this friend a growing awareness of their sin, and a growing realisation of their helplessness before the just and holy God.

THANKING GOD

> "For Christ also suffered once for sins, the righteous for the unrighteous..." (v 18).

Thank God for the wonderful truth that Jesus died for the unrighteous! Reflect on the way that he has saved you, even though you don't deserve it. Thank him that he stands ready to save your friend, even though they don't deserve it either.

FOR A RELATIONSHIP WITH GOD

> "... to bring you to God" (v 18).

Pray that God would bring your friend into a relationship with himself. Pray that your friend would be able to look forward to a day when they will meet him face to face in heaven.

A CHRISTIAN
FRIEND

1 JOHN 3 v 11-22

PEOPLE TO PRAY FOR:

_____

_____

_____

_____

Almighty Father, please give this friend...

OUTWARD-LOOKING LOVE

"We should love one another" (v 11).

Give thanks for this brother or sister in Christ, and for the love you have for each other. Then pray for your friend's relationships with other Christians in their church; that they would be filled with love for all God's people, and not just their close friends or the people they naturally click with. Ask that God would make your friend more and more loving.

A WILLINGNESS TO SUFFER

"Do not be surprised ... if the world hates you" (v 13).

Think through some of the ways and situations in which your brother or sister is facing hostility for their faith: perhaps it's a colleague who likes to pick a fight, or a family member who makes them the butt of every joke. Pray that your friend would always be willing to be hated by the world, just as the Lord Jesus was.

SACRIFICIAL LOVE

> *"Jesus Christ laid down his life for us. And we ought to lay down our lives for our brothers and sisters" (v 16).*

Praise God that Jesus was willing to lay down his life for us. Pray for yourself, that you would lay down your life for this friend; not out of selfish motives, but as an overflow of Christ's love. Prayerfully think about some sacrificial, practical ways in which you could do this.

 REST IN GRACE

> *"We set our hearts at rest in his presence" (v 19).*

Even when we know the doctrine of grace, often we still fall into the trap of trying to earn God's favour or forgiveness through our own effort. Pray that this friend would stop striving and rest in God's presence.

 CONFIDENCE IN PRAYER

> *"We have confidence before God and receive from him anything we ask" (v 21-22).*

Thank God that we can approach him confidently in prayer. Pray that your friend would regularly make time to pray confidently and listen humbly to God through his word. What concern is your friend praying for at the moment? Join them in praying for that thing now. Has your friend recently been disappointed by God's response to their prayers? Pray for faithful persistence and eyes that are always keen to see God at work.

A CHRISTIAN GOING THROUGH A HARD TIME

ROMANS 5 v 1-5

PEOPLE TO PRAY FOR:

_____

_____

_____

_____

As you bring this loved one before God, thank him for, and ask that he would increase, their...

 PEACE

> *"We have peace with God through our Lord Jesus Christ" (v 1).*

Christians already have peace with the most important Person in the universe—but how easy it is to forget this! Pray that your brother or sister in Christ would know and treasure this peace. Ask that they would always be able to rejoice in the wonder of the gospel, even as things in life seem to be going wrong.

 PERSEVERANCE

> *"We know that suffering produces perseverance..." (v 3).*

Pray that they, and you, would know this to be true—that rather than only looking for a way out of this hard time, they would be looking for how God is working through it. Pray most of all that they would be learning to persevere in their faith—that they would not doubt God's goodness, but cling to Jesus.

3 CHARACTER

"... perseverance, character [or proven character—HCSB translation]..." (v 4).

As your loved one's sanctification—the change to their character that God has been making over time—is put to the test, pray that it will be proved to be a genuine work of God's Spirit. Pray that this time would be a glorious testament to God's power to transform human hearts; and that your church family would be encouraged by seeing this power at work.

4 HOPE

"... and character, hope" (v 4).

Pray that this suffering would lead your loved one to put their hope solely in God. What else will this person be tempted to look to for security? (Their job? Their relationships? Their health?) Pray that as God uses suffering to strip away these things, your loved one would place all their hope on God and his grace.

5 LOVE

"God's love has been poured out into our hearts" (v 5).

Pray that as this person hopes in God more, they would know his love for them more deeply, feeling his tangible comfort. When things get tough, it's so easy to become introspective, brooding and bitter. But pray instead that this person's heart would overflow with love for those around them.

A CHRISTIAN
WHO IS SICK

2 CORINTHIANS
4 v 16 – 5 v 10

PEOPLE TO PRAY FOR:

_____

_____

_____

 SPIRITUAL RENEWAL

"Though outwardly we are wasting away, yet inwardly we are being renewed day by day" (4 v 16).

First and foremost, pray for this loved one's spiritual health. Ask that each day, God would give them renewed thankfulness; renewed trust in God's promises; renewed love for God's word; renewed resolve to fight sin; renewed desire to see Christ's church grow; and renewed concern for other Christians.

 FORWARD FOCUS

"We groan, longing to be clothed instead with our heavenly dwelling" (v 2).

When we are sick, we groan! But pray that in groaning, your loved one would also be increasingly looking forward to receiving their new body in the new creation, free from pain and sickness.

3 THANK GOD

"We groan and are burdened" (v 4).

Thank God that he hears your loved one's groans and understands their burdens. Cry out to God for healing.

4 UNSHAKEABLE CONFIDENCE

"Therefore we are always confident ... and would prefer to be away from the body and at home with the Lord" (v 6-8).

Pray that God would bless this brother or sister with deep, unshakeable assurance in the reality of heaven and Jesus' ability to guarantee their place there. Pray that your loved one would be comforted, knowing that, long or short, their earthly life will end with their arrival "home with the Lord". And pray that this assurance would give them a visible confidence as they undergo treatment, visits to the hospital, and so on.

5 THE RIGHT GOAL

"We make it our goal to please him" (v 9).

Difficult circumstances are a new opportunity to live in a way that pleases our Creator. Whether their illness is serious or minor—a lifelong condition or a two-day tummy bug—pray that this person would make pleasing God, rather than recovering, their number one goal. Pray that they would seize opportunities to respond to situations in a deliberately godly way.

A LOVED ONE WHO IS REJOICING

PSALM 103

PEOPLE TO PRAY FOR:

_____

_____

_____

_____

As you rejoice with this loved one, pray that they would...

PRAISE THE LORD

"Praise the LORD, my soul" (v 1).

Spend some time rejoicing with your loved one in prayer. Praise and thank God for the good thing that has happened and for the way that he has provided for them.

REMEMBER FORGIVENESS

"Forget not all his benefits—who forgives all your sins" (v 2-3).

Pray that this blessing would not cause your loved one to forget the best blessing that God offers: his forgiveness. Thank God that he doesn't offer partial forgiveness, but forgiveness in totality: "as far as the east is from the west, so far has he removed our transgressions from us" (v 12). If this person is a Christian, pray that they would remember to rejoice more over their salvation than any material gift that God gives.

REMEMBER GRACE

"He does not treat us as our sins deserve or repay us according to our iniquities" (v 10).

What makes any good thing all the more remarkable is that we don't deserve it! Thank God that although we don't deserve anything good from him, he graciously gives it anyway.

 ### REMEMBER WHAT LASTS

Pray that your loved one would remember that "the life of mortals is like grass" (v 15).

Pray that this person would remember that careers, new homes, holidays, spouses and children will only, at very best, last a lifetime; but they will not endure to eternity.

 ### DISCOVER EVERLASTING JOY

"From everlasting to everlasting the LORD's love is with those who fear him" (v 17).

Thank God that his people will enjoy his love for ever. Pray that this loved one would fear the Lord and so be able to look forward to greater, everlasting joys in heaven.

A CHRISTIAN
STRUGGLING
WITH SIN

ROMANS 6 v 1-14

PEOPLE TO PRAY FOR:

_____

_____

_____

_____

Father, please help this person to...

RESOLVE TO FIGHT

"We are those who have died to sin; how can we live in it any longer?" (v 2).

Thank God that, because of Christ, your friend has died to sin. Pray that they would appreciate the emptiness and illogicality of continuing to live in sin, and share Paul's commitment to battling it. Perhaps their resolve is flagging—ask that they would not grow weary, but would remember this truth.

LOOK FORWARD

"We will certainly also be united with [Christ] in a resurrection like his ... anyone who has died has been set free from sin" (v 5-7).

Thank God for the certainty of being raised with Christ. Pray that when your brother or sister is tempted, this would cause them to look forward with excitement to being perfected in Christ, and living free from temptation in the new creation.

ERADICATE SIN

> *"Do not offer any part of yourself to sin"*
> *(v 13).*

Think through the ways in which this person might be tempted to compromise with sin. Pray that they wouldn't settle for cutting down the amount they sin, but would strive to eradicate it completely.

 PURSUE RIGHTEOUSNESS

> *"Offer every part of yourself to [God] as an*
> *instrument of righteousness" (v 13).*

Often our struggle with a particular sin can define our walk with God; or it can wrongly become an all-consuming concern. Pray that your loved one wouldn't be so focused on stopping sinning that they forget to pursue righteousness and make themselves available to God, to serve him. Pray through some of the areas in which this friend is aiming positively to grow in godliness.

 REJOICE IN GOD'S GRACE

> *"You are not under the law, but under*
> *grace" (v 14).*

Thank God that our salvation does not rely on our ability to keep God's law, but on God's grace. Pray that your loved one would have great joy and assurance in this knowledge. Pray that both of you would be increasingly thankful for it.

A LOVED
ONE MAKING
A DECISION

ACTS 1 v 15-26

PEOPLE TO PRAY FOR:

 SEEK WISE ADVICE

"Peter stood up among the believers" (v 15).

Pray that this loved one would be seeking wise counsel as they make this decision. We can very easily—in our pride—want to make every decision on our own; equally we can easily—in our desire to please—listen to the wrong voices. Pray that your loved one wouldn't listen to worldly advice ("Do what makes you richest", "Do what makes you most comfortable", "Do what everyone else is doing"), even when it comes from the mouths of Christians. Pray instead that they would look for, and find, wise advice from mature believers.

 LOOK TO GOD'S WORD

"For ... it is written in the Book of Psalms..." (v 20).

Pray that as they read the Scriptures, God would be convicting this person of sinful desires or motivations, and giving them godly priorities. Ask that the Spirit would be working in their heart to bring all their priorities into line with God's priorities.

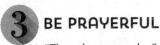

BE PRAYERFUL

"Then they prayed..." (v 24).

Pray that this person would pray! Ask God to use this experience to make this brother or sister more prayerfully dependent on him.

HAVE CONFIDENCE IN GOD'S SOVEREIGNTY

"'Lord, you know everyone's heart' ... Then they cast lots" (v 24, 26).

Thank our all-seeing God that he knows everything that is in our heart, and knows everything that is in our future. Pray that your loved one would have confidence and peace in the knowledge of God's sovereignty. Ask that they would be able to see this decision in perspective; even big decisions—like marriages, careers, homes and children—become small when compared to God's really, really big salvation plan.

MOVE FORWARD IN FAITH

"The lot fell to Matthias; so he was added" (v 26).

Pray that, in light of points 1 – 4, this person would be able to make a decision soon: trusting that God is guiding them and knowing that, in one sense, they cannot get it "wrong". Ask God to prevent them from being crippled by indecision, but instead to keep them moving forward in faith.

A LOVED ONE ON THEIR BIRTHDAY

2 THESSALONIANS 1 v 3-13

PEOPLE TO PRAY FOR:

_____

_____

_____

_____

On this loved one's birthday, pray...

THANKING GOD

"We ought always to thank God for you"
(v 3).

Thank God for this person and the relationship you enjoy with them. Praise God for the unique way in which he has made them, and for all the things you love about them: their personality, their talents, their hopes and dreams. Thank God for some of the happy times you have spent together in the last 12 months.

FOR GROWING FAITH

"Your faith is growing more and more" (v 3).

Wherever they're currently at spiritually, pray that on their next birthday, this person would be able to look back on the year and see how their faith has grown. Pray for growing faith in God's promises; growing faith in God's unchanging character; growing faith in the wisdom of God's word; and growing faith in Jesus' saving work on the cross.

FOR ABOUNDING LOVE

"The love all of you have for one another is increasing" (v 3).

Pray that your own love for this person would be increasing. Ask for strength to love them deeply, self-lessly and consistently. Pray for opportunities to put this love into action in practical, self-sacrificial ways.

THEY WOULD KNOW GOD

"He will punish those who do not know God … on the day he comes to be glorified in his holy people and to be marvelled at among all those who have believed" (v 8-10).

With each passing birthday, this person is one year closer to eternity. If they're not yet a Christian, pray that they would become one of God's "holy people". If your loved one is a Christian, pray that they would be joyfully looking forward to the day when they will see Jesus and marvel at him.

FOR INCREASING GOODNESS

Pray that God "may bring to fruition [their] every desire for goodness … so that the name of our Lord Jesus may be glorified in [them]" (v 11-12).

Pray that this person would desire goodness; and that the Lord Jesus would shine out through them more and more over the coming year.

A LOVED ONE
AT CHRISTMAS

LUKE 1 v 46-55

PEOPLE TO PRAY FOR:

Lord God, as we remember the gift of your Son at Christmas, please help this person to…

 REJOICE IN YOU

> *"My spirit rejoices in God my Saviour" (v 46).*

Perhaps your loved one is looking forward to Christmas with great anticipation; or maybe this season is sad or stressful for them. Whatever their situation, pray that their spirit would rejoice in the truth that Christ Jesus came into this world to save sinners.

 THANK YOU

> *"The Mighty One has done great things for me" (v 49).*

Think through the good things that God has done in this person's life this year, and thank God for each one. If they're a Christian, praise God for the greatest thing that he has done for them—giving them eternal life. Thank him for all the ways in which he has been growing this person in their faith over the last 12 months.

 **FEAR YOU**

"His mercy extends to those who fear him…" (v 50).

At a time of year when the focus is on Jesus as a cute baby in a manger, pray that this loved one would also have a right fear of God: one that leads them to recognise their own sinfulness, rely on God's mercy, and submit to Jesus as their Lord. Pray that they would find some spiritual headspace in the busyness that comes with Christmas to reflect on this.

 ENJOY FAMILY TIME

"… from generation to generation" (v 50).

Pray point 3 for your loved one's family, young and old, as they get together this Christmas. Perhaps your loved one is desperate to be an effective witness to unbelieving members of their family; boldly pray that the gospel would spread from "generation to generation"! Perhaps your loved one finds this extended time with their family difficult; pray that they would have a happy and peaceful time together.

 REMEMBER YOUR GOODNESS

"He has filled the hungry with good things" (v 53).

Thank God for the good food and good things we enjoy at Christmas time. Pray that your loved one would remember that all good things come from God, and thank him for them.

WHEN SOMEONE
YOU LOVE HAS DIED
TRUSTING IN CHRIST

1 THESSALONIANS 4 v 13-18

PEOPLE TO PRAY FOR:

_____

_____

_____

_____

Loving heavenly Father, please help me to...

 THANK YOU

> *"We do not want you to be uninformed about those who sleep in death" (v 13).*

Thank God that death is not the end; that Jesus can wake someone from death as easily as we would wake someone from sleep. Thank God that he will raise this person to new life, just as he has promised.

 HOLD ON TO HOPE

> *"Do not grieve like the rest of mankind, who have no hope" (v 13).*

No matter how badly you miss this person, or how big a void they have left in your life, thank God that you do have hope. Pray that you would keep this hope in view, even when the pain is immense. And pray for any non-Christian friends and family who are now grieving without hope; pray that your hope in the face of death would be a powerful witness to them.

LOOK BACK

"Jesus died and rose again" (v 14).

Thank God for Jesus' death: that because Christ faced God's wrath on the cross, your loved one will not face God's wrath. Then praise God for Jesus' resurrection. Thank him that this historical fact gives us certainty that those who are in Christ will also be raised from death. Pray that looking back at what Christ did would give you deep-rooted assurance and comfort.

 **LOOK FORWARD**

"We who are still alive and are left will be caught up together with them in the clouds to meet the Lord in the air" (v 17).

Thank God for all that this person meant to you. Then thank him that though for now you are separated from them, you will see them again on the day that Christ returns. And thank God that—even sweeter than this reunion—you and your loved one will meet Jesus face to face and "be with the Lord for ever".

 ENCOURAGE OTHERS

"Therefore encourage one another with these words" (v 18).

Pray that God would help you to be an encouragement to others, even as you are grieving. Pray that you would be looking to the needs of others and seeking to meet them.

WHEN A LOVED ONE HAS DIED NOT TRUSTING IN CHRIST

ROMANS 8 v 26-27
AND 11 v 33-36

PEOPLE TO PRAY FOR:

_____

_____

_____

_____

Loving heavenly Father, please help me to...

REMEMBER THAT THE SPIRIT PRAYS

"We do not know what we ought to pray for, but the Spirit himself intercedes for us through wordless groans" (8 v 26).

At times like this, it's hard to know what to say to God; we want to come to our Father in prayer, but we're lost for words. Or sometimes we can't even bring ourselves to try. But thank God that even when we don't know what to pray, and even when we don't want to pray, the Spirit is speaking to the Father on our behalf anyway.

THANK YOU

Thank God that he's the one "who searches our hearts" (v 27).

Maybe you can't put into words how you're feeling right now; but be comforted because God knows without you having to tell him.

TRUST YOU

Recognise that God's judgments are "unsearchable ... and his paths beyond tracing out" (11 v 33).

We cannot possibly understand them. But thank God that he is the judge, and not you. Pray that you would be able to trust him in that.

KEEP FROM BITTERNESS

"Who has ever given to God, that God should repay them?" (v 35).

Meditate on this verse and ask God to keep you from feeling bitter or angry towards him.

SEEK YOUR GLORY

"To him be the glory for ever! Amen" (v 36).

Ask God to help you to remember that it's his glory that matters most. Ask him to enable you to keep loving him and aiming to bring glory to him, even at this really difficult time.

ALSO AVAILABLE IN THE RANGE:

If we want God to be at work in our church, we pray. But so often our prayers for our church can feel shallow, repetitive and stuck in a rut.

That's where this little book will help: each section takes a passage of Scripture and suggests five things to pray for your church family. Because when we pray in line with God's priorities as found in his word, our prayers are powerful—they really change things.

THEGOODBOOK.CO.UK/5THINGSCHURCH

thegoodbook
COMPANY
Opening up the Bible

At The Good Book Company, we are dedicated to helping Christians and local churches grow. We believe that God's growth process always starts with hearing clearly what he has said to us through his timeless word—the Bible.

Ever since we opened our doors in 1991, we have been striving to produce resources that honour God in the way the Bible is used. We have grown to become an international provider of user-friendly resources to the Christian community, with believers of all backgrounds and denominations using our Bible studies, books, evangelistic resources, DVD-based courses and training events.

We want to equip ordinary Christians to live for Christ day by day, and churches to grow in their knowledge of God, their love for one another, and the effectiveness of their outreach.

Call us for a discussion of your needs or visit one of our local websites for more information on the resources and services we provide.

Your friends at The Good Book Company

UK & EUROPE
NORTH AMERICA
AUSTRALIA
NEW ZEALAND

 thegoodbook.co.uk
thegoodbook.com
thegoodbook.com.au
thegoodbook.co.nz

 0333 123 0880
866 244 2165
(02) 6100 4211
(+64) 3 343 2463

 WWW.CHRISTIANITYEXPLORED.ORG
Our partner site is a great place for those exploring the Christian faith, with a clear explanation of the good news, powerful testimonies and answers to difficult questions.